Value-Stream Mapping Workshop

Participant Guide

By Mike Rother and John Shook
Foreword by Jim Womack and Dan Jones

A Learning Solution from LEI

Lean Enterprise Institute, Inc.
Boston, MA, USA
lean.org

Lean Enterprise Institute

ISBN: 978-0-9667843-8-1
Design by Off-Piste Design

Lean Enterprise Institute, Inc.
Boston, MA 02210 USA
617-871-2900 (fax) 617-871-2999
lean.org

Contents

Whenever there is a product for a customer,
there is a value stream.
The challenge lies in seeing it.

Foreword

by Jim Womack and Dan Jones

Welcome to the *Value-Stream Mapping Workshop*. This participant guide was designed to help you follow along with your facilitator through the workshop, and to provide you with information that helps clarify some of the terminology and techniques used in it.

The workshop itself follows on the heels of the book by Mike Rother and John Shook called *Learning to See: Value-Stream Mapping to Add Value and Eliminate Muda.* This book has been a complete success, winning a Shingo Research Award, and outselling even our most optimistic forecasts. When it was confirmed that these techniques were proven valuable to any organization wishing to become leaner, it became evident to us through the many requests for training that we couldn't personally visit everyone who was interested. Instead we have focused our efforts on the creation of a workshop that can be facilitated by experienced trainers in organizations around the globe.

The workshop is called *Value-Stream Mapping* because these mapping techniques allow you to see the sources of waste in your value streams. However, mapping does not in itself offer any value to your customers. So when you leave this session, we hope that you have not only learned the techniques, but that you will actually use them to quickly change your organization for the better.

For those of you that have been exposed to lean thinking in the past you may be familiar with the vital steps that are required as you start down the road to eliminate waste ...

1. Find a change agent (how about you?)
2. Get the knowledge or find a sensei (a teacher whose learning curve you can borrow)
3. Seize (or create) a crisis or lever to motivate action across your firm
4. Map the future state for your product families
5. Pick something important and get started removing waste quickly, to surprise yourself with how much you can accomplish in a very short period

This workshop is designed to help you through steps four and five in a logical step-by-step fashion.

As with any of the products of the Lean Enterprise Institute, we'd like to know what you think about this workshop. Your feedback helps us to design products that have relevancy and value. You can send your feedback directly to us at info@lean.org

We sincerely hope that you find the following two days to be enjoyable and interesting. Best wishes as you embark on your own lean journey!

Jim Womack and Dan Jones
Cambridge, MA, USA and
Little Birch, Hereford, UK
February 2000

How to Use this Participant Guide

Dear Participant,

We've tried to develop the contents of this participant guide in a way that will enhance your learning experience. The framework of the modules in this guide matches the learning framework that you will be using in class.

Each module starts with a picture of the learning framework, explaining to you where you are in the course content, where you've been, and where you are going. This will help you to see the flow of the course, and to internalize the content into your own mental framework.

All of the instructor's slides have been included from each session. Beneath each slide is an area for you to take notes, and write down comments. When it comes to working on the Acme case studies and practical exercises, there are blank mapping sheets that you can use to work along with the instructor.

At the end of each module, we've included a short quiz. Each quiz is in multiple-choice format, and helps you determine whether you've understood the main points of the module. Don't be bashful! If you haven't understood something, then speak up. The chances are that someone else didn't understand, too!

In the final sections of this participant guide, there is a glossary that defines terms used in this course, a summary of the mapping icons, further reading references, and a survey that will help us to improve this workshop.

We hope this guide helps you to enjoy the workshop!

Sincerely,

The Lean Enterprise Institute Staff

Learning Framework

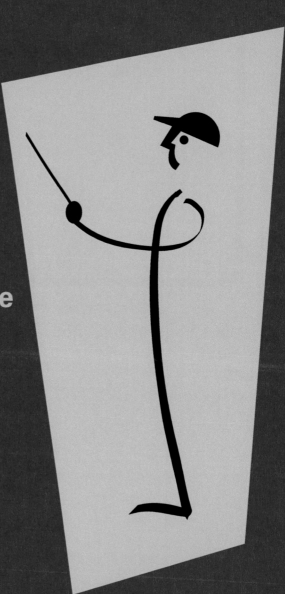

Training to See
A Value-Stream Mapping Workshop

Purpose:

1. Introduce value-stream mapping in a hands-on manner.

2. Develop your ability to "see the flow" and design future-state value streams.

VSM Workshop

Workshop Introduction

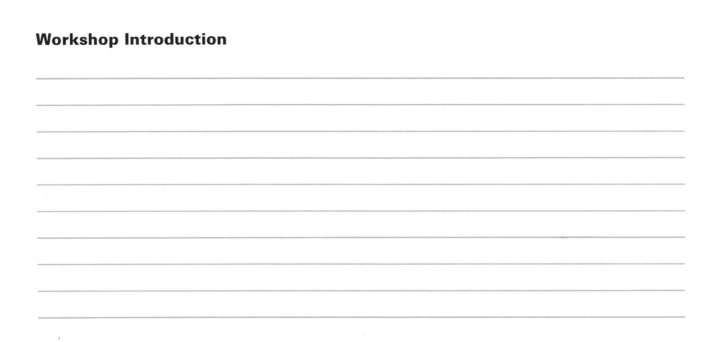

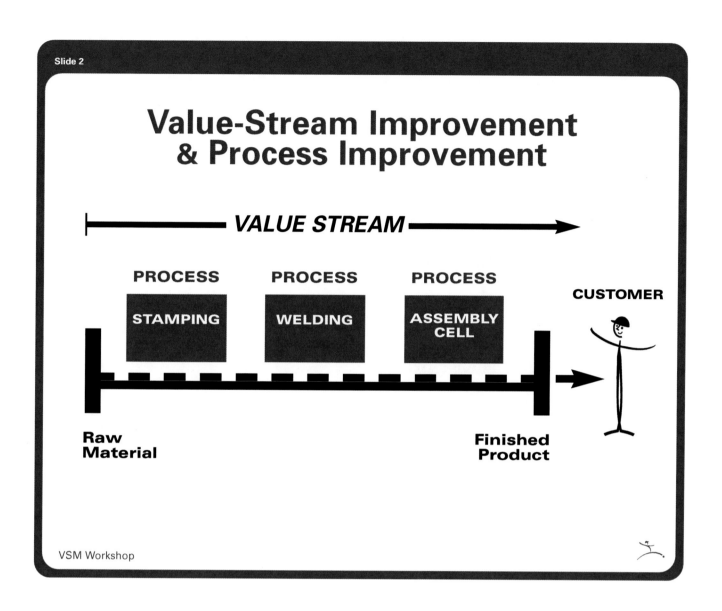

Defining Value Stream

_____

_____

_____

_____

_____

_____

_____

_____

_____

Value-Stream Mapping

A) Follow a product's production path from <u>beginning to end</u>, and draw a <u>visual representation</u> of every process in the <u>material & information flows</u>.

B) Then draw (using icons) a "future-state" map of how value should flow.

VSM Workshop

Defining Value-Stream Mapping

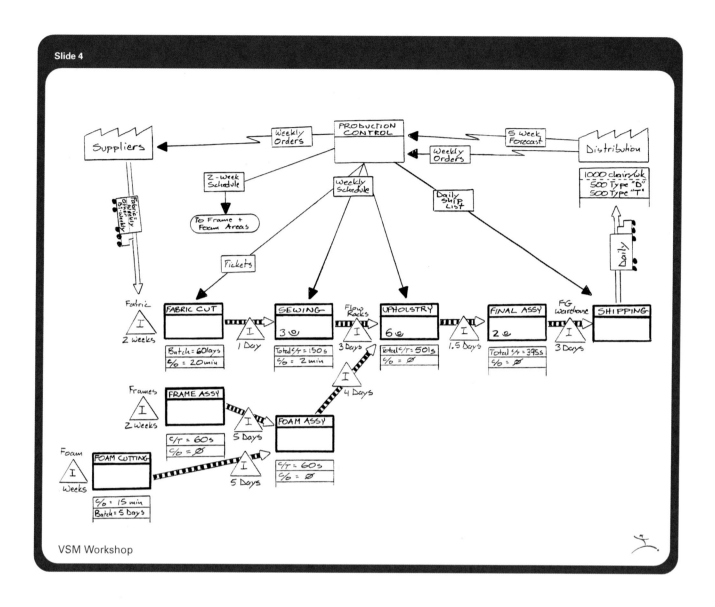

VSM Workshop

Sample Value-Stream Map

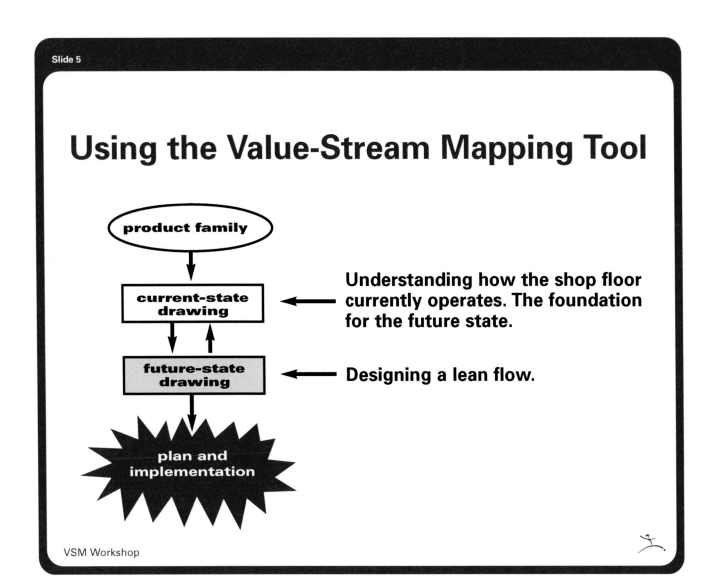

Using the Value-Stream Mapping Tool

product family

current-state drawing

Understanding how the shop floor currently operates. The foundation for the future state.

future-state drawing

Designing a lean flow.

plan and implementation

VSM Workshop

Mapping Steps

Focus on one product family

Determine Product Families via:

Similar downstream "assembly" steps and equipment

		Process Steps & Equipment						
		Spot Weld	Robot Weld	Flash Remove	Paint	Manual Assm.	Fixtures Assm.	Electronic Test
PRODUCTS	LH Steering Bracket	X		X	X	X		
	RH Steering Bracket	X		X	X	X		
	Instrument Panel Brace		X				X	X
	Seat Rail	X					X	
	Bumper Brackets	X				X	X	

Product Family

Value-Stream Managers
Each Value Stream Needs a Value-Stream Manager

For product ownership beyond functions

Assign responsibility for future-state mapping and implementing lean value streams to line managers with the capability to make change happen across functional and departmental boundaries.

Value-stream managers should make their progress reports to the top manager on site.

VSM Workshop

The Value-Stream Manager

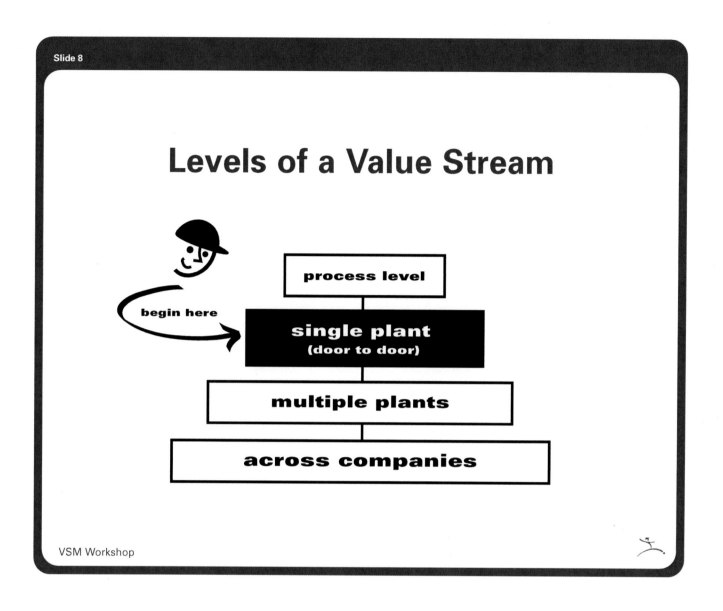

Levels of a Value Stream

- process level
- **single plant (door to door)**
- multiple plants
- across companies

begin here

VSM Workshop

Starting at the "Door-to-Door" Level

Session 1 Quiz

Multiple choice; circle the best answer.

1. Value-stream mapping looks at:

A. The people, material, and information flow in a value stream.

B. The material and information flows in a value stream.

C. The detailed operation steps within cells.

D. The steps that people take in designing and producing a product.

2. A product family matrix is used to:

A. Create a listing of all your products and the steps that are taken to produce them.

B. Decide which products are most important to your customers.

C. Identify and group products into families based on whether they pass through similar steps in your downstream processes.

D. Divide the mapping teams up into groups with individual mapping assignments.

3. A value-stream manager:

A. Is a staff person vested with the authority to make change in the value stream.

B. Is a lead hand with the responsibility for understanding a product family's value stream and improving it.

C. Is responsible for the day-to-day operation of the processes in the value-stream plant.

D. Is a line person reporting to the senior person on site, with the lead responsibility for understanding a product family's value stream and improving it.

Learning Framework

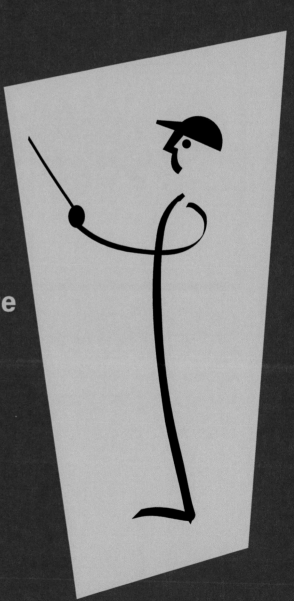

1. Introduction & Getting Started

2. The Current-State Map

   Exercise 1: Current State

3. Lean Value Stream

4. The Future-State Map

   Exercise 2: Future State

5. Achieving the Future State

6. Conclusion

Current-State Drawing

product family

current-state drawing

future-state drawing

plan and implementation

Understanding how the shop floor currently operates

✓ Material and information flows

✓ Draw using icons

✓ Start with the "door-to-door" flow

✓ Have to walk the flow and get actuals
  • No standard times
  • Draw by hand, with pencil

✓ Foundation for the future state

VSM Workshop

The Current-State Map

"ACME Stamping" Data Set

Acme Stamping Company produces several components for vehicle assembly plants. This case concerns one product family: a steel instrument-panel bracket subassembly in two types: one each for left-hand and right-hand drive versions of the same automobile model. These components are sent to the State Street Vehicle Assembly Plant (the customer).

CUSTOMER REQUIREMENTS:
- **18,400 pieces per month**
  12,000 per month of Type "LH"
  6,400 per month of Type "RH"
- **Customer plant operates on two shifts**
- **Palletized returnable tray packaging with 20 brackets in a tray and up to 10 trays on a pallet. The customer orders in multiples of trays.**
- **One daily shipment to the assembly plant by truck**

WORK TIME:
- **20 days in a month**
- **Two-shift operation in all production departments**
- **Eight (8) hours every shift, with overtime if necessary**
- **Two 10-minute breaks during each shift**
  Manual processes stop during breaks
  Unpaid lunch

Acme Stamping Case Review

"ACME Stamping" Data Set (continued)

PRODUCTION PROCESSES:

- Acme's process for this product family involves stamping a metal part followed by welding and subsequent assembly. The components are then staged & shipped to the vehicle assembly plant on a daily basis.
- Switching between Type "LH" (left-hand drive) and Type "RH" (right-hand drive) brackets requires 1-hour changeover in stamping and 10-minute fixture change in the welding processes.
- Steel coils are supplied by Michigan Steel Co.
  Deliveries are made to Acme on Tuesdays and Thursdays.

ACME PRODUCTION CONTROL DEPARTMENT:

- Receives State Street's 90/60/30-day forecasts and enters them to MRP
- Issues Acme 6-week forecast to Michigan Steel Co. via MRP
- Secures coil steel by weekly faxed order release to Michigan Steel Co.
- Receives daily firm order from State Street
- Generates MRP-based weekly departmental requirements based upon customer order, WIP inventory levels, F/G inventory levels, and anticipated scrap and downtime
- Issues weekly build schedules to Stamping, Welding, and Assembly processes
- Issues daily shipping schedule to Shipping Department

Production Process Review

"ACME Stamping" Data Set (continued)

PROCESS INFORMATION:
All processes occur in the following order and each piece goes through all processes.

1) STAMPING
(The press makes parts for many Acme products)
- **Automated 200-ton press with coil** (automatic material feed)
- **Cycle time: 1 second** (60 pieces per minute)
- **Changeover time: 1 hour** (good piece to good piece)
- **Machine reliability: 85%**
- **Observed inventory:**
  5 days of coils before stamping
  4,600 pieces of Type "LH" finished stampings
  2,400 pieces of Type "RH" finished stampings

2) SPOT-WELD WORKSTATION I
(dedicated to this product family)
- **Manual process with one operator**
- **Cycle time: 39 seconds**
- **Changeover time: 10 minutes** (fixture change)
- **Reliability: 100%**
- **Observed inventory:**
  1,100 pieces of Type "LH"
  600 pieces of Type "RH"

3) SPOT-WELD WORKSTATION II
(dedicated to this product family)
- **Manual process with one operator**
- **Cycle time: 46 seconds**
- **Changeover time: 10 minutes** (fixture change)
- **Reliability: 80%**
- **Observed inventory:**
  1,600 pieces of Type "LH"
  850 pieces of Type "RH"

4) ASSEMBLY WORKSTATION I
(dedicated to this product family)
- **Manual process with one operator**
- **Cycle time: 62 seconds**
- **Changeover time: none**
- **Reliability: 100%**
- **Observed inventory:**
  1,200 pieces of Type "LH"
  640 pieces of Type "RH"

5) ASSEMBLY WORKSTATION II
(dedicated to this product family)
- **Manual process with one operator**
- **Cycle time: 40 seconds**
- **Changeover time: none**
- **Reliability: 100%**
- **Observed finished-goods inventory**
  in warehouse:
  2,700 pieces of Type "LH"
  1,440 pieces of Type "RH"

6) SHIPPING DEPARTMENT
**Removes parts from finished-goods
warehouse and stages them for truck
shipment to customer.**

Material

ASSEMBLY

Process Box

XYZ
Corporation

Customer

| C/T = 45 sec. |
| C/O = 30 min |
| 3 Shifts |
| 2% Scrap |

Data Box

$\boxed{I}$

300 pieces / 1 Day
Inventory

Mon.
+ Wed.

Shipment

PUSH

**Finished Goods
to Customer**

max. 20 pieces
—FIFO►

**First-In-First-Out
Sequence Flow**

**Super-
market**

C **Pull**

Material Info. Flow

Electronic Info. Flow

Weekly
Schedule

Information

Production Kanban

Withdrawal Kanban

**Signal
Kanban**

**Kanban
Post**

**Kanban Arriving
in Batches**

$\boxed{O \; X \; O \; X}$

Load Leveling

$6o^{\prime}$

"Go-See" Scheduling

weld
changeover

Kaizen Burst

$\odot$

Operator

Session 2 Quiz

Multiple choice; circle the best answer.

1. The best way to draw a value-stream map is:

A. In pencil on the work floor, mapping the whole value stream yourself.

B. In your office with a good drawing software package.

C. In pencil, by dividing the value stream into segments, and assigning each segment to a different mapping team.

D. In pencil, on the work floor using standard times obtained from engineering.

2. Lead time is:

A. The total time of those work elements that actually transform the product in a way that the customer is willing to pay for.

B. The time it takes one piece to move all the way through a process or a value stream from start to finish.

C. The time it takes an operator to go through all of his or her work elements before repeating them.

D. The total time it takes inventory to be depleted from a finished-goods warehouse.

3. Data boxes should contain information based on:

A. Engineered standards.

B. The average measurement for a fiscal year.

C. The measurement on an ideal day.

D. What you observe as you draw your map.

Team Tips
Current-State Mapping

1 MAPPING THE CURRENT STATE:

- <u>Review the basic processing</u> steps and <u>calculate the assembly takt time</u> in your team's breakout room.
- <u>Everyone draw</u> while on the shop floor.
  Be sure to <u>draw both the material & information flows</u>.
- Always <u>introduce yourself</u> to operators and tell them what you are doing: "Drawing the total factory flow as part of a training session." Show them your drawings.
- <u>Select a scribe</u> and <u>combine your drawings</u> into one current-state map (in team area).
- Calculate <u>total lead time versus processing time</u>.
- Draw the map on a "presentation sheet" and select presenters.

2 PRESENTING YOUR CURRENT-STATE MAP:

- <u>All team members</u> go up front with presenter. State the product family and takt.
- Present from your presentation sheet. (Less than 5 minutes.)
- Start with the customer and information flow into the facility.
- State the lead time vs. processing time.
- What are the problems you see? Where did you find push and overproduction?
- Share any future-state thoughts you have so far.

VSM Workshop

VSM Team Tips: Current-State Mapping

Material

Process Box

ASSEMBLY

Customer

XYZ Corporation

Data Box

| C/T = 45 sec. |
| C/O = 30 min |
| 3 Shifts |
| 2% Scrap |

Inventory

300 pieces / 1 Day

Shipment

Mon. + Wed.

PUSH

Finished Goods to Customer

First-In-First-Out Sequence Flow

max. 20 pieces

—FIFO►

Super-market

Pull

Material Info. Flow

Electronic Info. Flow

Information

Weekly Schedule

Production Kanban

Withdrawal Kanban

Signal Kanban

Kanban Post

Kanban Arriving in Batches

Load Leveling

OX OX

"Go-See" Scheduling

Kaizen Burst

weld changeover

Operator

Learning Framework

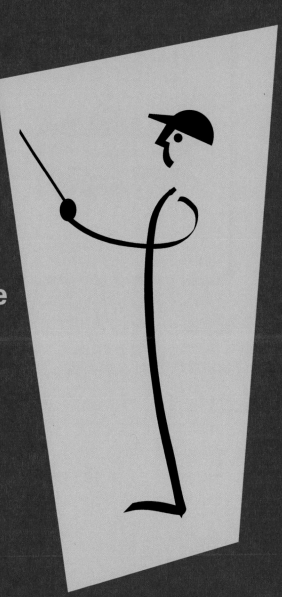

Future-State Drawing

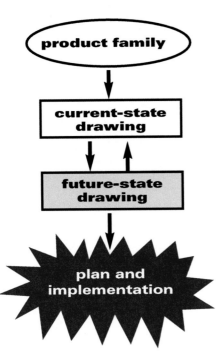

Designing a Lean Flow

- **The power behind value-stream mapping is you always need a future state!**

- **70% and keep updating. <u>Use pencil</u>!**

- **Material and information flows**

- **Basis for your work plan—like a "blueprint"**

- **Begin by drawing on current state**

- **1st iteration assumes existing steps & equipment**
  Can move equipment, combine, take out conveyors, make minor purchases, etc.

 But there is a problem!

The Future State

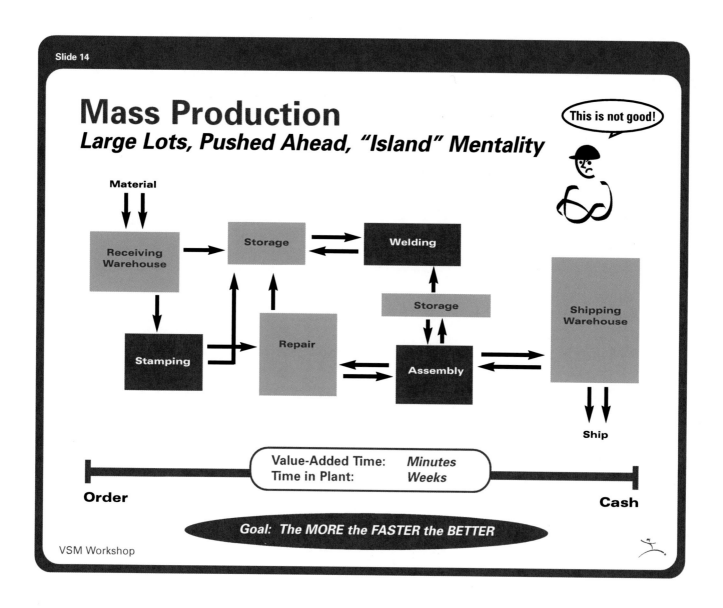

Mass Production
Large Lots, Pushed Ahead, "Island" Mentality

VSM Workshop

What's Wrong with Acme's Value Stream?

Waste

- *The elements of production that add no value to the product*
- *Waste only adds cost and time*

Things to Remember about Waste

- **Waste is really a symptom, rather than a root cause of the problem.**

- **Waste points to problems within the system (at both process and value-stream levels).**

- **We need to find and address causes of waste.**

VSM Workshop

Waste

Overproduction

= Making more than is required by the next process
= Making earlier than is required by the next process
= Making faster than is required by the next process

Overproduction

Individual Efficiency vs. System Efficiency

How fast should we produce?

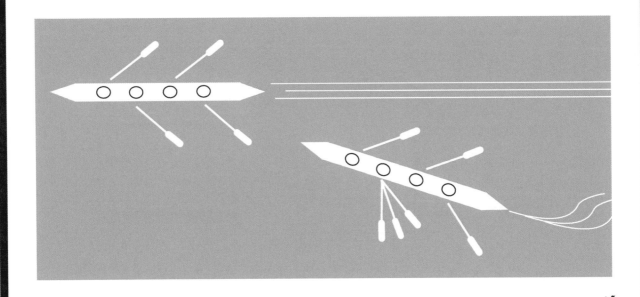

VSM Workshop

System Efficiency

_____

_____

_____

_____

_____

_____

_____

_____

_____

Takt Time

Synchronizes pace of assembly to match pace of sales.

Rate for assembling a product based on sales rate.

$$\text{Takt Time} = \frac{\text{Effective Working Time per Shift}}{\text{Customer Requirement per Shift}}$$

$$\frac{27,600 \text{ sec}}{460 \text{ pieces}} = 60 \text{ sec}$$

Takt Time and Cycle Time

Cycling Faster than Takt Time
Operator Balance Chart

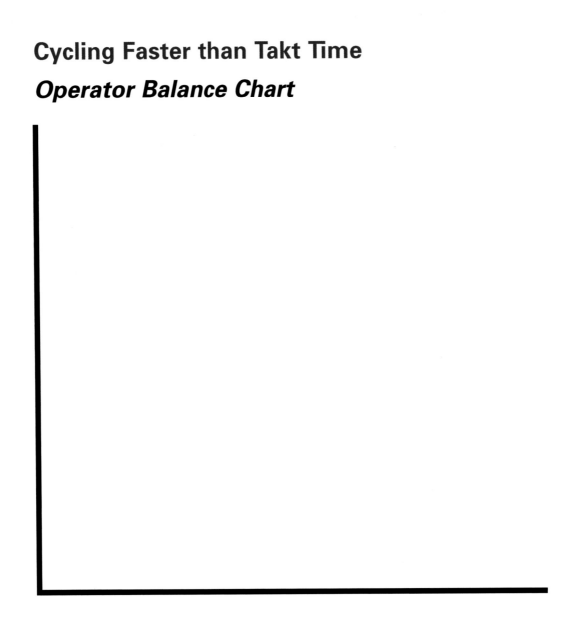

Build to Supermarket or to Shipping?

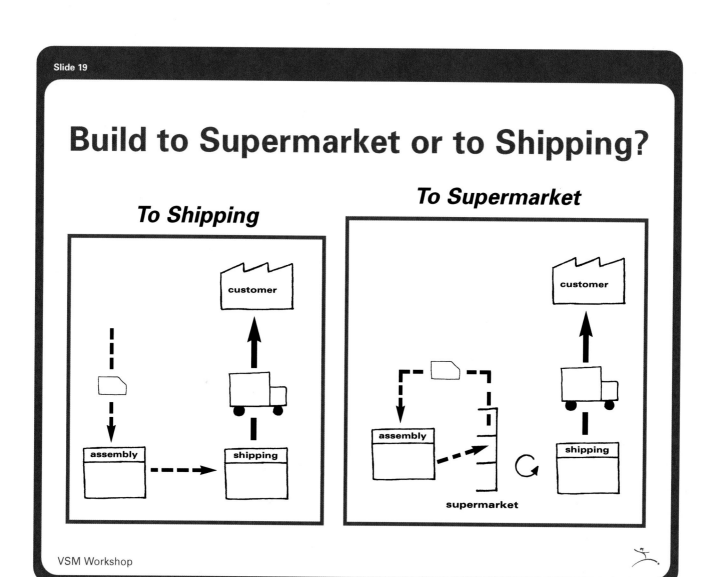

Holding Finished Goods

Continuous-Flow Processing

Batch & Push Processing

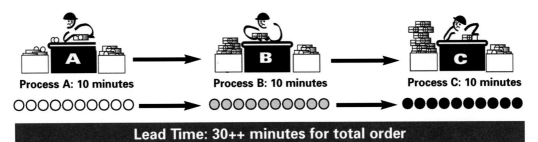

Process A: 10 minutes   **Process B: 10 minutes**   **Process C: 10 minutes**

Lead Time: 30++ minutes for total order

Continuous Flow "make one, move one"

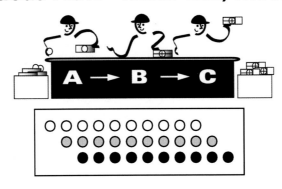

VSM Workshop

Continuous Flow Processing

Problem Points in the Flow
Where One-Piece Flow Ends

How can we control production between flows?
MRP-based schedules?

Where Continuous Flow Stops

Supermarket Pull System

1) Customer process goes to supermarket and withdraws what it needs when it needs it.

2) Supplying process produces to replenish what was withdrawn.

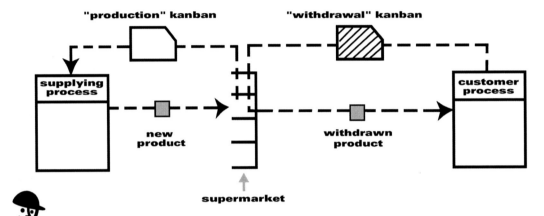

Purpose: **A way to control production between flows.**
Controls production at supplying process without trying to schedule.

VSM Workshop

Supermarket Pull Systems

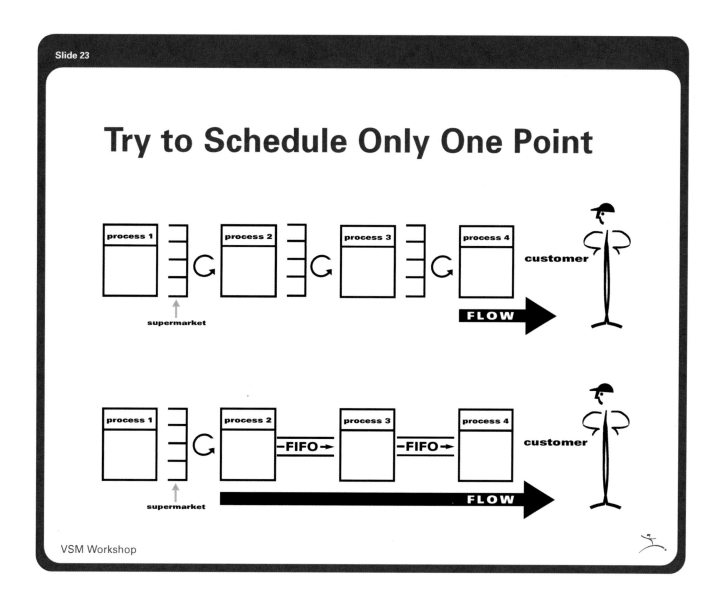

Try to Schedule Only One Point

Mixed Production at the Pacemaker
(Assembly)

No Good

Assembly Schedule

Monday .... 400 A
Tuesday .... 100 A, 300 B
Wednesday ... 200 B, 200 C
Thursday ...... 400 C
Friday .... 200 C, 200 A

orders | Stamping Dept.

Important:
Near-zero changeover time and frequent changeovers at the pacemaker process!

Better: Every Part Every Day

Monday: 140 A, 100 B, 160 C

Even Better: Every Part Every Ship Window

Monday ⟶

| 50B | 70A | 80C | 50B | 70A | 80C |

VSM Workshop

Mixed Production

_____

_____

_____

_____

_____

_____

_____

_____

_____

What Happens to a Lean Flow...

...if a machine breaks down?
...if a defective part is included with good parts?

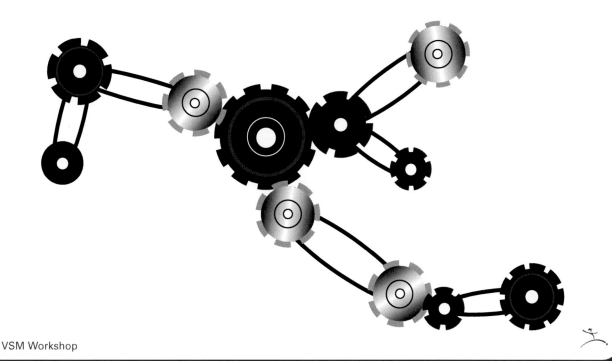

VSM Workshop

What Happens When Problems Occur?

Paced Withdrawal at the Pacemaker

- **What amount of work do you schedule and take away at the pacemaker?**
- **This amount = your management time frame.**
  (How often do you know your performance to customer demand?)
- **Are you providing takt image?**

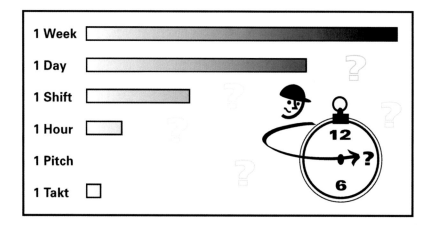

VSM Workshop

Management Time Frame

Session 3 Quiz

Multiple choice; circle the best answer.

1. Takt time is:

A. The customer demand rate.

B. The rate at which the sales departments plan to sell products to customers based on promotions.

C. The fastest rate at which your individual operations can produce the products.

D. The average amount of product bought by your customers in a week.

2. A supermarket is used where:

A. Processes are close together but have different cycle times.

B. A customer requires specialized products from a finished-goods warehouse.

C. Continuous flow is not possible due to distance, unreliability, or where processes serve multiple product families.

D. Pull can be implemented throughout the door-to-door value stream.

3. A pacemaker process:

A. Ensures that all processes downstream are controlled by supermarket pull systems.

B. Receives its products from supermarkets controlled by MRP systems.

C. Is always a bottleneck, requiring constant supervision and staff adjustment.

D. Responds to the external customer, and is usually the point at which production is scheduled in the door-to-door value stream.

Learning Framework

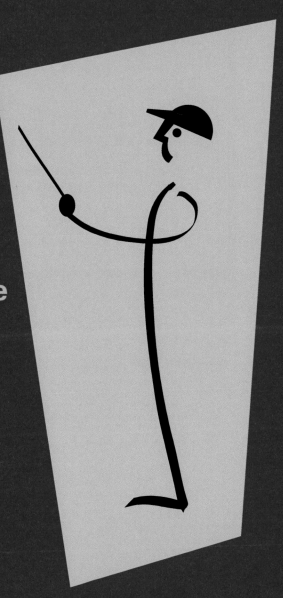

Future-State Questions

☐ **What is the takt time?**

☐ **Will we build to shipping or to a supermarket?**

☐ **Where can we use continuous flow?**

☐ **Where do we have to use supermarket pull systems?**

☐ **At what single point in the production chain do we trigger production?**

☐ **How do we level the production mix at the pacemaker process?**

☐ **What increment of work will we release and take away at the pacemaker process? (Leveling the volume)**

SUPPORTING IMPROVEMENTS

☐ **What process improvements will be necessary? (e.g., uptime, changeover, training)**

VSM Workshop

Starting the Future State

_____

_____

_____

_____

_____

_____

_____

_____

_____

_____

Future-State Icons

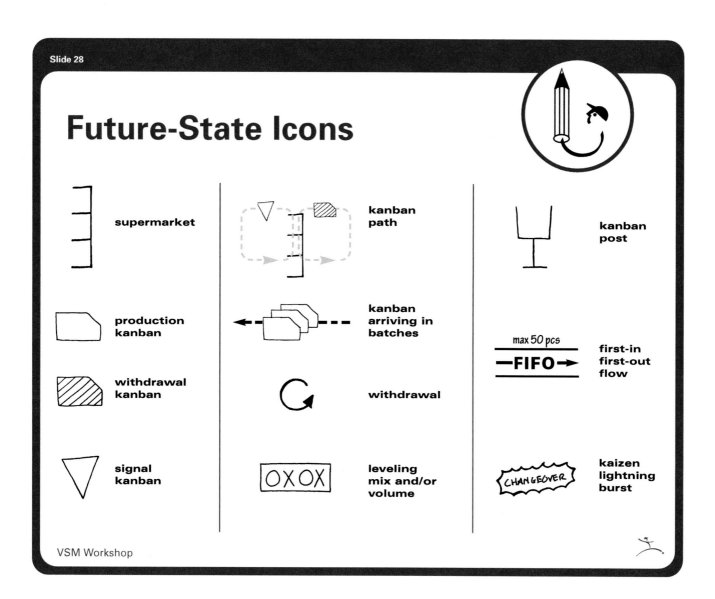

supermarket	kanban path	kanban post
production kanban	kanban arriving in batches	first-in first-out flow (max 50 pcs, FIFO)
withdrawal kanban	withdrawal	
signal kanban	leveling mix and/or volume (OXOX)	kaizen lightning burst (CHANGEOVER)

Future-State Icons

Material

Process Box

Customer

| C/T = 45 sec. |
| C/O = 30 min |
| 3 Shifts |
| 2% Scrap |

Data Box

300 pieces / 1 Day
Inventory

Mon.
+ Wed.
Shipment

PUSH

**Finished Goods
to Customer**

max. 20 pieces
─FIFO►
**First-In-First-Out
Sequence Flow**

**Super-
market**

Pull

Material Info. Flow

Electronic Info. Flow

| Weekly
Schedule |

Information

Production Kanban

Withdrawal Kanban

**Signal
Kanban**

**Kanban
Post**

**Kanban Arriving
in Batches**

| O X | O X |

Load Leveling

"Go-See" Scheduling

weld
changeover
Kaizen Burst

Operator

Where is Continuous Flow Possible?
Acme Current State

Where is Continuous Flow Possible?
Acme Future State

Session 4 Quiz

Multiple choice; circle the best answer.

1. Kanban cards are used to:

A. Improve flow by providing a working instruction to the next operator.

B. Control the size of a FIFO lane so that inventory doesn't build.

C. Allow the operators to sort the cards into "right-sized" batches to minimize changeovers.

D. Provide an instruction that regulates the sequence and timing of production.

2. When calculating takt time:

A. Include lunches and breaks in the available working time and reduce them afterwards.

B. Include lunches and breaks but do not include planned machine downtime.

C. Do not include lunches and breaks, but include machine downtime as available working time.

D. Do not include lunches and breaks, machine downtime, and any other unavailable production time.

Team Tips
Future-State Mapping

1 **MAPPING THE FUTURE STATE:**
- Use the list of future-state questions.
- Begin by drawing on copies of your current-state map.
- Then draw a future-state map.
- Make a slide or presentation sheet.

2 **PRESENTING YOUR FUTURE-STATE MAP:**
- Present from your slide or presentation sheet.
- Explain the following, including your rationale:
  - <u>Takt?</u>
  - <u>Build to order or supermarket?</u>
  - Where will you <u>flow</u>? Where do you need to *pull*?
  - What is the pacemaker process?
  - What is the <u>schedule point</u> and <u>pitch</u>?
  - Will you level the assembly mix?
  - Are <u>supporting improvements necessary</u>?
  - Resulting <u>lead-time improvement</u>

VSM Workshop

VSM Team Tips: Future-State Mapping

Material

Process Box
ASSEMBLY

Customer
XYZ Corporation

Data Box

| C/T = 45 sec. |
| C/O = 30 min |
| 3 Shifts |
| 2% Scrap |

Inventory
300 pieces / 1 Day

Shipment
Mon. + Wed.

PUSH

Finished Goods to Customer

First-In-First-Out Sequence Flow
max. 20 pieces
—FIFO►

Super-market

Pull

Material Info. Flow

Electronic Info. Flow

Information
Weekly Schedule

Production Kanban

Withdrawal Kanban

Signal Kanban

Kanban Post

Kanban Arriving in Batches

Load Leveling
OXOX

"Go-See" Scheduling

Kaizen Burst
weld changeover

Operator

Learning Framework

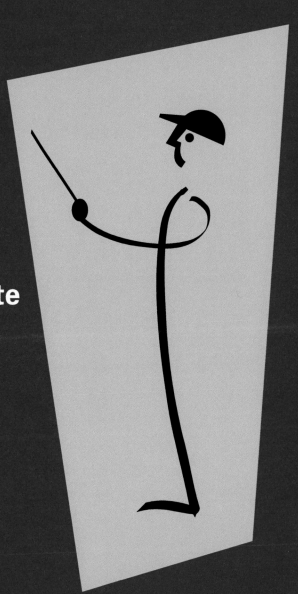

A Plan to Get There

Implementation

- *Don't Wait!*
- *To "manage the exceptions" you need a plan!*
    1. **Tie it to business objectives.**
    2. **Break your future state into "loops."**
    3. **Make a Value-Stream Plan: what to do by when.**
    4. **Now relate the FS Map to your layout.**
    5. **VS Manager completes VS Review form in advance.**
    6. **Conduct VS Reviews walking the flow.**

VSM Workshop

Future-State Implementation

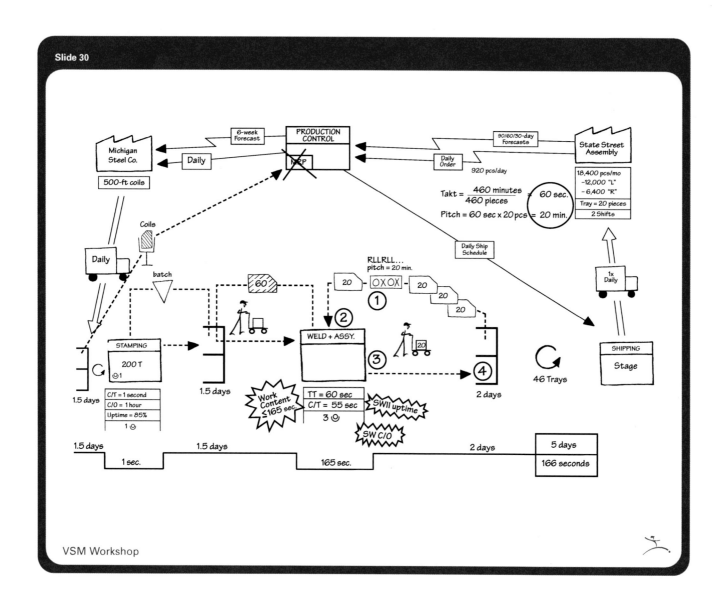

Value-Stream Loops

Date																				**Signatures**			
Facility Manager				**Yearly Value-Stream Plan**														Plant Manager	Union	Engineering	Maintenance		
V.S. Manager																							

Product-Family Business Objective	V.S. loop	Value-Stream Objective	Goal (measurable)	Monthly Schedule												PERSON IN CHARGE	RELATED INDIVIDUALS & DEPTS	REVIEW SCHEDULE	
				1	2	3	4	5	6	7	8	9	10	11	12			Reviewer	Date

	Product Family	

VSM Workshop

Value-Stream Plan

PLANT-LEVEL OBJECTIVE	V.S. loop	OBJECTIVE & MEASURABLE GOAL	PROGRESS CONDITIONS	EVALUATION	REMAINING PROBLEMS	POINTS AND IDEAS FOR COMING YEAR'S OBJECTIVES

Date

Facility Manager

V.S. Manager

Signatures

Value-Stream Review

◯ = SUCCESS △ = LIMITED SUCCESS ✕ = UNSUCCESSFUL

Product Family:

VSM Workshop

Value-Stream Review

Session 5 Quiz

Multiple choice; circle the best answer.

1. Creating value-stream loops helps you to:

A. Break your total value-stream plan into manageable pieces and prioritize them.

B. Communicate your plan to senior management.

C. Assign kaizen teams to be responsible for each loop.

D. Develop measures for each loop based on improving lead times.

2. Improvements to a value stream often follow the pattern:

A. Kaizen first, then implement pull and flow.

B. Implement flow first, then kaizen, then implement leveling and pull.

C. Implement leveling first, then kaizen to implement pull.

D. Develop flow, then pull where flow isn't possible, then level production.

3. The point of value-stream mapping is:

A. To document your current state for future reference.

B. To create a future-state diagram.

C. To implement a future state with less waste.

D. To reduce staffing in the production environment.

Learning Framework

Training to See
A Value-Stream Mapping Workshop

Purpose:

1. Introduce value-stream mapping in a hands-on manner.

2. Develop your ability to "see the flow" and design future-state value streams.

VSM Workshop

Workshop Objectives

Implementation via Kaizen

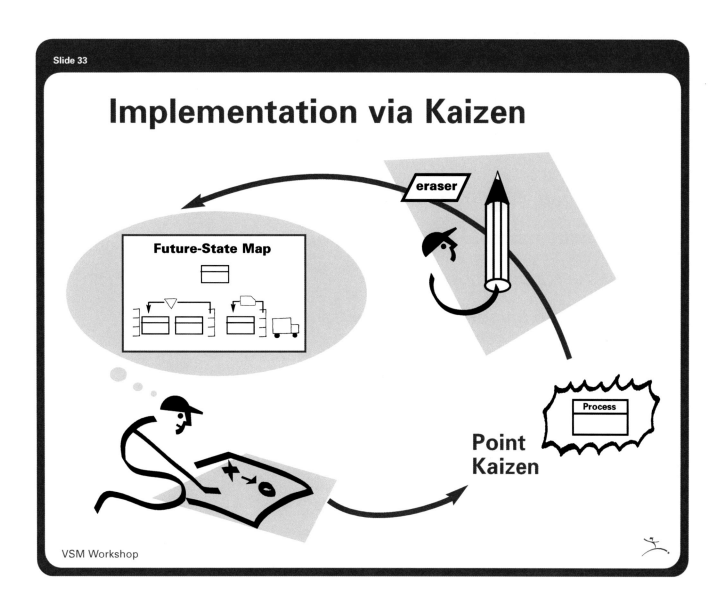

VSM Workshop

Implementation via Kaizen

Value-Stream Mapping

- *Helps you visualize more than the single process level*

- *Links the material and information flows*

- *Provides a common language*

- *Provides a blueprint for implementation*

- *More useful than quantitative tools*

- *Ties together lean concepts and techniques*

stamping ········· welding ········· assembly ······►

VSM Workshop

Summary of Value-Stream Mapping Benefits

Batch-and-Queue

A mass-production approach to operations in which large lots (batches) of items are processed and moved to the next process—regardless of whether they are actually needed—where they wait in a line (a queue).

Cell

The location of processing steps for a product immediately adjacent to each other so that parts, documents, etc., can be processed in very nearly continuous flow, either one at a time or in small batch sizes that are maintained through the complete sequence of processing steps. A "U shape" is common because it minimizes walking distance and allows different combinations of work tasks for operators. This is an important consideration in lean production because the number of operators in a cell will change with changes in demand. A U shape also facilitates perfor-mance of the first and last steps in the process by the same operator, which is helpful in maintaining work pace and smooth flow. Many companies use the terms cell and line interchangeably.

Changeover

The process of switching from the production of one product or part number to another in a machine (e.g., a stamping press or molding machine) or a series of linked machines (e.g., an assembly line or cell) by changing parts, dies, molds, fixtures, etc. (Also called a setup.) Changeover time is measured as the time elapsed between the last piece in the run just completed and the first good piece from the process after the changeover.

Continuous Flow

Producing and moving one item at a time (or a small and consistent batch of items) through a series of processing steps as continuously as possible, with each step making just what is requested by the next step. Continuous flow can be achieved in a number of ways, ranging from moving assembly lines to manual cells. It is also called one-piece flow, single-piece flow, and make one, move one.

Cycle Time

How often a part or product is completed by a process, as timed by observation. This time includes operating time plus the time required to prepare, load, and unload. Operator cycle time is the time it takes an operator to complete all the work elements at a station before repeating them, as timed by direct observation.

Every Product Every Interval (EPEx)

The frequency with which different part numbers are produced in a production process or system. If a machine is changed over in a sequence so that every part number assigned to it is produced every three days, then EPEx is three days. In general, it is good for EPEx to be as small as possible in order to produce small lots of each part number and minimize inventories in the system.

Fabrication Processes

Segments of the value stream that respond to requirements from internal customers. Fabrication processes often are characterized by general-purpose equipment that changes over to make a variety of components for different processes. Compare to pacemaker process.

First In, First Out (FIFO)

The principle and practice of maintaining precise production and conveyance sequence by ensuring that the first part to enter a process or storage location is also the first part to exit. (This ensures that stored parts do not become obsolete and that quality problems are not buried in inventory.) FIFO is a necessary condition for pull system implementation. The FIFO sequence is often maintained by a painted lane or physical channel that holds a certain amount of inventory. The supplying process fills the lane from the upstream end while the customer process withdraws from the downstream end. If the lane fills up, the supplying process must stop producing until the customer consumes some of the inventory.

Flow Production

The production system Henry Ford introduced at his Highland Park, MI, plant in 1913. The objective of flow production was to drastically reduce product throughput time and human effort through a series of innovations. These included consistently interchangeable parts so that cycle times could be stable for every job along an extended line, the line itself, the reconfiguration of part fabrication tasks so that machines were lined up in process sequence with parts flowing quickly and smoothly from machine to machine, and a production control system ensuring that the production rate in parts fabrication matched the consumption rate of parts in final assembly.

Heijunka

Leveling the type and quantity of production over a fixed period of time. This enables production to efficiently meet customer demands while avoiding batching and results in minimum inventories, capital costs, manpower, and production lead time through the whole value stream.

Just-in-Time (JIT) Production

A system of production that makes and delivers just what is needed, just when it is needed, and just in the amount needed. JIT and jidoka are the two pillars of the Toyota Production System. JIT relies on heijunka as a foundation and is comprised of three operating elements: the pull system, takt time, and continuous flow. JIT aims for the total elimination of all waste to achieve the best possible quality, the lowest possible cost and use of resources, and the shortest possible production and delivery lead times. The idea for JIT is credited to Kiichiro Toyoda, the founder of Toyota Motor Corporation, during the 1930s.

Kaizen

Continuous improvement of an entire value stream or an individual process to create more value with less waste. There are two levels of kaizen. System or flow kaizen focuses on the overall value stream. This is kaizen for management. Process kaizen focuses on individual processes. This is kaizen for work teams and team leaders. Value-stream mapping is an excellent tool for identifying an entire value stream and determining where flow and process kaizen are appropriate.

Kanban

A kanban is a signaling device that gives authorization and instructions for the production or withdrawal (conveyance) of items in a pull system. The term is Japanese for "sign" or "signboard." Kanban have two functions in a production operation: They instruct processes to make products and they instruct material handlers to move products. The former use is called production kanban (or make kanban), the latter use is termed withdrawal kanban (or move kanban).

Material Handling

Moving necessary materials through a production process within a facility. In a lean production system, material handling does much more than just deliver materials. A lean material-handling system can serve as the primary means of carrying production instructions. A well-designed system can improve the efficiency of production operators by taking away wasteful activities such a getting materials, wrestling with dunnage, and reaching for parts.

Material Requirements Planning (MRP)

A computerized system typically used to determine the quantity and timing requirements for delivery and production of items. Using MRP specifically to schedule production at processes in a value stream results in push production because any predetermined schedule is only an estimate of what the next process will need. Manufacturing Resource Planning, often called MRP II, expands MRP to include capacity planning, a finance interface to translate operations planning into financial terms, and a simulation tool to assess alternative production plans.

Milk Run

A method to speed the flow of materials between facilities by routing vehicles to make multiple pickups and drop-offs at many facilities. By making frequent pickups and drop-offs with milk run vehicles connecting a number of facilities rather than waiting to accumulate a truckload for direct shipment between two facilities, it is possible to reduce inventories and response times along a value stream.

Muda

Any activity that consumes resources without creating value for the customer. Within this general category it is useful to distinguish between type one muda, consisting of activities that cannot be eliminated immediately, and type two muda, consisting of activities that can be eliminated quickly through kaizen.

Overproduction

Producing more, sooner, or faster than is required by the next process. It is considered the most grievous form of waste because it generates and hides other wastes, such as inventories, defects, and excess transport.

Paced Withdrawal

The practice of releasing production instructions to work areas and withdrawing completed product from work areas at a fixed, frequent pace. This practice can be used as a means of linking material flows with information flow. Paced withdrawal serves to prevent overproduction and quickly alerts managers if there is a production problem.

Pacemaker Process

Any process along a value stream that sets the pace for the entire stream. (The pacemaker process should not be confused with a bottleneck process, which necessarily constrains downstream processes due to a lack of capacity.) The pacemaker process is usually near the customer end of the value stream, often the final assembly cell. However, if products flow from an upstream process to the end of the stream in a FIFO sequence, the pacemaker may be at this upstream process.

Pitch

The amount of time needed in a production area to make one container of products. The formula for pitch is: takt time x pack-out quantity = pitch.

Product Family

A product and its variants passing through similar processing steps and common equipment just prior to shipment to the customer. The significance of product families for Lean Thinkers is that they are the unit of analysis for value-stream maps, which are defined from the most downstream step just before the customer.

Pull Production

A method of production control in which downstream activities signal their needs to upstream activities. Pull production strives to eliminate overproduction and is one of the three major operating elements of a complete just-in-time production system along with takt time and continuous flow.

Queue Time

The time a product spends waiting in line for the next processing step.

Supermarket

The location where a predetermined standard inventory is kept to supply downstream processes. Supermarkets are ordinarily located near the supplying process to help that process see customer usage and requirements.

Takt Time

The available production time divided by customer demand. For example, if a widget factory operates 480 minutes per day and customers demand 240 widgets per day, takt time is two minutes. If customers want two new products per month, takt time is two weeks. The purpose of takt time is to precisely match production with demand. It provides the heartbeat of a lean production system.

Value

The inherent worth of a product as judged by the customer and reflected in its selling price and market demand. The value in a typical product is created by the producer through a combination of actions, some of which produce value as perceived by the customers and some of which are merely necessary given the current configuration of the design and production process. The objective of Lean Thinking is to eliminate the latter class of activities while preserving or enhancing the first set.

Value-Creating Time

The time spent on any activity that the customer judges of value. A simple test for whether a task and its time is value-creating is to ask if the customer would judge a product less valuable if this task could be left out without affecting the product. For example, rework and queue times are unlikely to be judged of any value by customers, while actual design and fabrication steps are.

Value Stream

All of the actions, both value-creating and nonvalue-creating, required to bring a product from concept to launch and from order to delivery. These include actions to process information from the customer and actions to transform the product on its way to the customer.

Value-Stream Loops

Segments of a value stream whose boundaries are typically marked by supermarkets. Breaking a value stream into loops is a way to divide future-state implementation into manageable pieces.

Value-Stream Manager

An individual assigned clear responsibility for the success of a value stream. The value stream may be defined on the product or business level (including product development) or on the plant or operations level (from raw materials to delivery.) The value-stream manager is the architect of the value stream, identifying value as defined from the customer's perspective, and leading the effort to achieve an ever-shortening value-creating flow.

Value-Stream Mapping (VSM)

A simple diagram of every step involved in the material and information flows needed to bring a product from order to delivery. Value-stream maps can be drawn for different points in time as a way to raise consciousness of opportunities for improvement. A current-state map follows a product's path from order to delivery to determine the current conditions. A future-state map deploys the opportunities for improvement identified in the current-state map to achieve a higher level of performance at some future point.

Waste

Any activity that consumes resources but creates no value for the customer.

Work-in-Process (WIP)

Items between processing steps within a facility. In lean systems, standardized work-in-process is the minimum number of parts (including units in machines) needed to keep a cell or process flowing smoothly.

Value-Stream Mapping Icons

Material Icons	Represents	Notes
ASSEMBLY	Process	One process box equals an area of flow. All processes should be labeled. Also used for departments, such as Production Control.
XYZ Corporation	Outside sources	Used to show customers, suppliers, and outside manufacturing processes.
C/T = 45 sec. C/O = 30 min 3 Shifts 2% Scrap	Data box	Used to record information concerning a manufacturing process, department, customer, etc.
I 300 pieces 1 Day	Inventory	Count and time should be noted.
Mon. + Wed.	Truck shipment	Note frequency of shipments.
▰▰▰▶	Movement of production material by PUSH	Material that is produced and moved forward before the next process needs it; usually based on a schedule.
⇒	Movement of finished goods to the customer	
⊐⊐⊐	Supermarket	A controlled inventory of parts that is used to schedule production at an upstream process.

Material Icons	Represents	Notes
	Withdrawal	Pull of materials, usually from a supermarket.
max. 20 pieces —FIFO→	Transfer of controlled quantities of material between processes in a "First-In-First-Out" sequence	Indicates a device to limit quantity and ensure FIFO flow of material between processes. Maximum quantity should be noted.

Information Icons	Represents	Notes
←	Manual information flow	For example, production schedule or shipping schedule.
←	Electronic information flow	For example, via electronic data interchange (EDI).
Weekly Schedule	Information	Describes an information flow.
20	Production kanban (dotted line indicates kanban path)	The "one-per-container" kanban. Card or device that tells a process how many of what can be produced and gives permission to do so.
(hatched kanban icon)	Withdrawal kanban	Card or device that instructs the material handler to get and transfer parts (i.e., from a supermarket to the consuming process).
▽	Signal kanban	The "one-per-batch" kanban. Signals when a reorder point is reached and another batch needs to be produced. Used where supplying process must produce in batches because changeovers are required.

Information Icons	Represents	Notes
	Kanban post	Place where kanban are collected and held for conveyance.
	Kanban arriving in batches	
OXOX	Load leveling	Tool to intercept batches of kanban and level the volume and mix of them over a period of time.
	"Go see" production scheduling	Adjusting schedules based on checking inventory levels.

General Icons	Represents	Notes
weld changeover / welder uptime	Kaizen lightning burst	Highlights improvement needs at specific processes that are critical to achieving the value-stream vision. Can be used to plan kaizen workshops.
	Buffer or safety stock	"Buffer" or safety stock must be noted.
	Operator	Represents a person viewed from above.

References and Further Reading

If you'd like to find out more about lean, we suggest:

Books

Lean Thinking: Banish Waste and Create Wealth in Your Corporation, by Jim Womack and Dan Jones.

Lean Lexicon: A Graphical Glossary for Lean Thinkers, by The Lean Enterprise Institute.

Learning to See: Value-Stream Mapping to Add Value and Eliminate Waste, by Mike Rother and John Shook.

Creating Continuous Flow: An Action Guide for Managers, Engineers, and Production Associates, by Mike Rother and Rick Harris.

Making Materials Flow: A Material Handling Guide for Operations, Production-Control, and Engineering Professionals, by Rick Harris, Chris Harris and Earl Wilson.

Creating Level Pull: A Production-System Improvement Guide for Production-Control, Operations, and Engineering Professionals, by Art Smalley.

Seeing the Whole Value Stream, by Dan Jones and Jim Womack.

The Machine that Changed the World, by Jim Womack, Dan Jones, and Daniel Roos.

The Evolution of a Manufacturing System at Toyota, by Takahiro Fujimoto.

The Toyota Production System: Beyond Large-Scale Production, by Taiichi Ohno.

From the American System to Mass Production, 1800–1932, by David Hounshell.

A Study of the Toyota Production System from an Industrial Engineering Viewpoint, by Shigeo Shingo.

The Toyota Production System, by Yasuhiro Monden.

The New Manufacturing Challenge: Techniques for Continuous Improvement, by Kiyoshi Suzaki.

Harvard Business Review Articles

From Lean Production to the Lean Enterprise, by Jim Womack and Dan Jones. Product #94211.

The Lean Service Machine, by Cynthia Karen Swank. Product #R0310J.

Decoding the DNA of the Toyota Production System, by Steven Spear and H. Kent Bowen. Product #99509.

Beyond Toyota: How to Root Out Waste and Pursue Perfection, by Jim Womack and Dan Jones. Product #96511.

Learning to Lead at Toyota, by Steven Spear. Product #R0405E.

Web: lean.org

LEI's website is a free and rich resource of content. It offers a wide range of helpful tools and information to support improvement efforts in any setting.

Acme Current-State Map

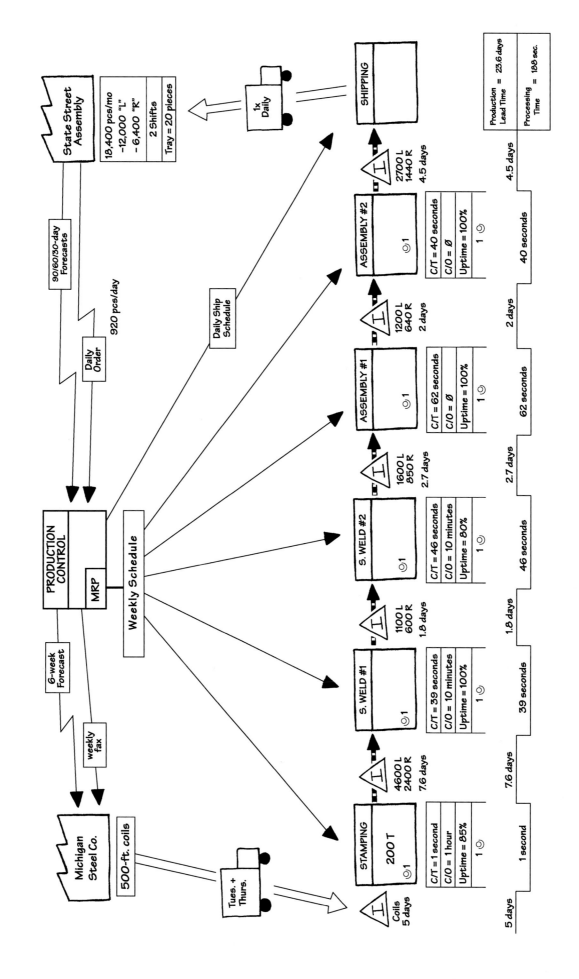

Acme Future-State Map

State Street Assembly

18,400 pcs/mo
  –12,000 "L"
  – 6,400 "R"

Tray = 20 pieces
2 Shifts

90/60/30-day Forecasts

920 pcs/day

Daily Order

$$Takt = \frac{460\ minutes}{460\ pieces} = 60\ sec.$$

$$Pitch = 60\ sec \times 20 pcs = 20\ min.$$

Daily Ship Schedule

PRODUCTION CONTROL

MRP

6-week Forecast

Daily

Michigan Steel Co.

500-ft coils

Coils

batch

Daily

STAMPING

200 T

C/T = 1 second
C/O = 1 hour
Uptime = 85%
1

1.5 days

1 sec.

RLLRLL...
pitch = 20 min.

OXOX

1   20

2   20

20 20 20

WELD + ASSY.

TT = 60 sec
C/T = 55 sec
3

Work Content ≤165 sec.

SWII uptime

SW C/O

3

4

2 days

46 Trays

SHIPPING

Stage

1x Daily

1.5 days   1.5 days   165 sec.   2 days

1 sec.   1.5 days   165 sec.   2 days   5 days

166 seconds

A Value-Stream Mapping Workshop Survey

Name: _____

Date: _____

In the spirit of continuous improvement, we would like to have feedback about this training so that it may be improved for the next session. Please write brief responses to the questions asked below in the spaces provided. Once complete, return your survey to the facilitator. Thank you.

Course Material

1. Do you feel confident in applying the techniques to your workplace immediately upon your return to work? If not, in which area(s) do you think you need more exposure to the concepts?

   _____

   _____

   _____

2. Did you feel that the material was clear and concise? In what ways do you feel we could improve the explanations or examples?

   _____

   _____

   _____

3. Was enough time spent on each module? Which modules did we spend too much time on? In which did we not spend enough time?

   _____

   _____

   _____

4. Did you find the participant guide to be clear and concise? How would you improve it?

   _____

   _____

   _____

   _____

   _____

   _____

Presentation

5. Did the instructor(s) speak clearly throughout the workshop? How could they improve the presentation the next time?

_____

_____

_____

6. Did the instructor(s) make sure to involve everyone in the workshop? Did you feel that you were given enough opportunity to participate and express your views?

_____

_____

_____

Classroom

7. Was the class size conducive to learning? What do you think is the optimal class size for this course?

_____

_____

_____

8. Was the classroom set-up conducive to the learning experience? How would you rate the classroom amenities?

_____

_____

_____

9. Did the communication prior to your attendance prepare you for what actually occurred in the workshop?

_____

_____

_____

Final Comments

10. Do you feel you received good value from this workshop? Why or why not?

_____

_____

_____

Thank you for your comments. They will be used to improve future sessions.

Lean Enterprise Institute

Continue Your Learning

The Lean Enterprise Institute (LEI) has a wide range of learning resources, all with the practical knowledge you need to sustain a lean transformation:

Learning Materials

Our plain-language books, workbooks, leadership guides, and training materials reflect the essence of lean thinking—*doing*. They draw on years of research and real-world experiences from lean transformations in manufacturing and service organizations to provide tools that you can put to work immediately.

Education

Faculty members with extensive implementation experience teach you actual applications using case studies, work sheets, formulas, and methodologies you need for implementation. Select from courses that address coaching, culture change, senior management's roles, technical topics, and much more.

Events

Every March the Lean Summit explores the latest lean concepts and case studies, presented by executives and implementers. Other events focus on an issue or industry, such as starting a lean transformation or implementing lean in healthcare. Check *lean.org* for details and to get first notice of these limited-attendance events.

lean.org

A quick and secure sign-up delivers these online learning resources:

- Use of the Connection Center to network or benchmark with fellow Lean Thinkers.

- Entry to a range of Forums where you can ask questions or help others.

- First notice about LEI events, webinars, and new learning materials.

About the Lean Enterprise Institute

The Lean Enterprise Institute, Inc. was founded in 1997 by management expert James P. Womack, Ph.D., as a nonprofit research, education, publishing, and conferencing company. As part of its mission to advance lean thinking around the world, LEI supports the Lean Global Network (leanglobal.org), the Lean Education Academic Network (teachinglean.org), and the Healthcare Value Network (createvalue.org).

64048400R00046